BOOK BUDDIES

T0014361

don't talk to me while i'm reading!

duopress

an imprint of 🟦 sourcebooks

Books let you escape
into dream worlds.

I READ PAST
MY BEDTIME

Sleep Is Nice, But Books Are Better

It takes only six minutes of reading before bed to reduce stress levels by 68 percent, according to a University of Sussex study. That's better than listening to music, drinking a warm beverage, or taking a walk. And while your eyes perform the repetitive pattern of scanning a page and your brain is busied with the task of focusing, your body might just drift off to sleep more easily!

**YOU FELL
ASLEEP
HERE.**

midnight
reader

early morning
page-turner

propped on pillows

lunch break quick picker-upper

flat on a desk

balanced on
a living being

weekend warrior

weeknight
ritual-keeper

with a hands-free
book weight

on an e-reader

Pick an audiobook when...

→ you need to multitask

→ you're commuting

→ you'd like background noise

→ you want to enjoy storytelling

Read a hard copy...

→ for improved memory and cognition

→ to retain information

→ to focus your attention

→ to keep and love your books forever

Check out a digital book...

→ to have access to a world of books in a tiny space

→ to carry big tomes with you everywhere

I'm not antisocial...
I just prefer
books to people.

please...
DON'T TALK
TO ME
WHILE I'M
READING!

Reading:
helping introverts
avoid conversation
for centuries.

Do you know the answers to these literary history questions?

a) What was the first novel ever written?

b) Where was the first paper made?

c) What was the first book printed on Johannes Gutenberg's movable type press (around 1455)?

(Turn the page to see if you're right!)

READING IS THE BEST WAY TO TIME TRAVEL.

Answers:

a) *The Tale of Genji*, by Murasaki Shikibu, is thought to be the first modern novel.

b) Modern paper made of plant pulp was invented during the Han dynasty in China, around 200 BCE. Papyrus was first created in Egypt in the third millennium BCE.

c) The Bible (in Latin)—more than 150 copies were made and only 20 remain.

That feeling when:

→ You miss your subway stop because your nose was in a book.

→ You're late because you were finishing a chapter.

→ You don't know where the day went because you spent all of it reading.

→ You have a huge TBR pile and go to the bookstore anyway.

JUST. ONE. MORE. CHAPTER.

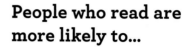

People who read are more likely to...

→ live longer

→ have nuanced perspectives from reading about other people and places

→ sleep better

→ have lower blood pressure and heart rate

→ build a broader vocabulary

→ feel less stressed

→ have improved memory and concentration

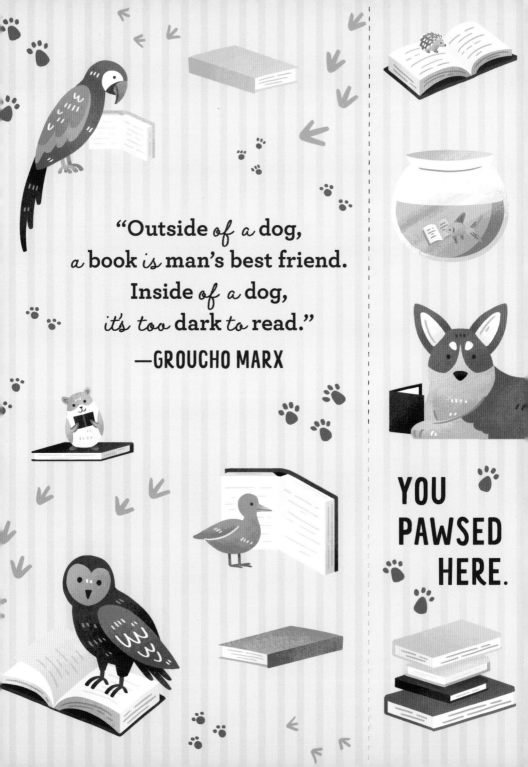

"Outside *of* *a* dog,
a book *is* man's best friend.
Inside *of* *a* dog,
it's *too* dark *to* read."
—GROUCHO MARX

YOU
PAWSED
HERE.

Plenty of famous authors relied on furry (and feathery) companions to help them write. Here are just a few:

→ Stephen King is a long-time fan of corgis and has been writing alongside them for decades.

→ E. B. White brought his dog Minnie to his office at the *New Yorker*.

→ Amy Tan's Yorkies go with her everywhere—even to book events!

→ Ian Fleming wrote *Goldeneye* in the company of two dogs.

→ Alice Walker's memoir, *The Chicken Chronicles*, tells of her life loving and being inspired by her flock of chickens.

→ Charles Dickens sometimes weaved mention of his raven, named Grip, into his books. Grip is perhaps also the inspiration for Edgar Allen Poe's famous poem "The Raven."

The Longest Books Ever Published

The Guinness World Record holder:

In Search of Lost Time or *Remembrance of Things Past* by Marcel Proust

Word count: 1,267,069

Also considered the longest novel:

Artamène ou le Grand Cyrus by Georges and/or Madeleine de Scudéry

Word count: 1,954,300

I LIKE BIG BOOKS AND I CANNOT LIE

If you only read *the* books *that* everyone else *is* reading, you can only think *what* everyone else *is* thinking.

—HARUKI MURAKAMI

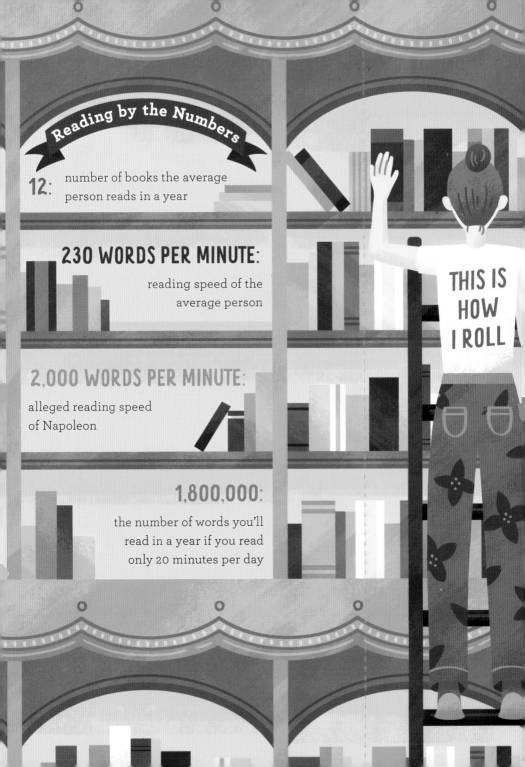

Reading by the Numbers

12: number of books the average person reads in a year

230 WORDS PER MINUTE: reading speed of the average person

2,000 WORDS PER MINUTE: alleged reading speed of Napoleon

1,800,000: the number of words you'll read in a year if you read only 20 minutes per day

THIS IS HOW I ROLL

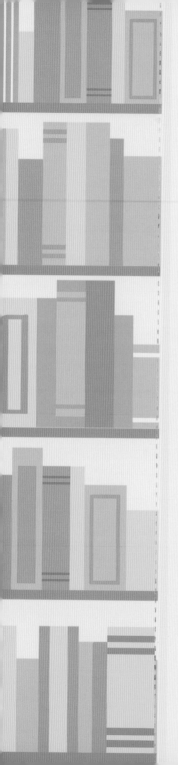

"Sometimes *you* just
need *to* lay *on the* couch *and*
read *for a* couple *of* years."
—UNKNOWN

Do you know these famous first lines from books?

a) Call me Ishmael.

b) Happy families are all alike; every unhappy family is unhappy in its own way.

c) You better not never tell nobody but God.

d) It was inevitable: the scent of bitter almonds always reminded him of the fate of unrequited love.

e) It was a dark and stormy night.

(Check your answers on the back!)

DON'T JUDGE A BOOK *by its* COVER— *it's what's* INSIDE *that* COUNTS.

Answers:

a) *Moby-Dick*, Herman Melville

b) *Anna Karenina*, Leo Tolstoy

c) *The Color Purple*, Alice Walker

d) *Love in the Time of Cholera*,
   Gabriel García Márquez

e) *A Wrinkle in Time*, Madeleine L'Engle

"Books are a uniquely portable magic."

—STEPHEN KING

It's called "librarian" because "book wizard" isn't an official job title.

Libraries House More Than Just Books!

→ More than 100 sourdough starters are preserved—and regularly fed—in the world's only sourdough library in St. Vith, Belgium.

→ Two libraries in Portugal employ bats as book preservationists—they eat insects that might damage books, and have been doing so for centuries. Library staff cover tables with fabric to make guano cleanup easier.

(continued on next page)

I HAVE NO SHELF CONTROL

YOU SEE ME ROLLIN'

Libraries House More Than Just Books! (cont'd)

➔ Vantaa, Finland, is home to a library with a karaoke room—the Tikkurila Library. Luckily, the room is soundproof.

➔ The Svalbard Global Seed Vault in Norway is a government-founded bank of genetic material from plants and crops around the world. It has room to save 4.5 million seed varieties from extinction.

SHHHHH,
I'M READING

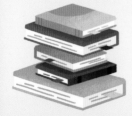

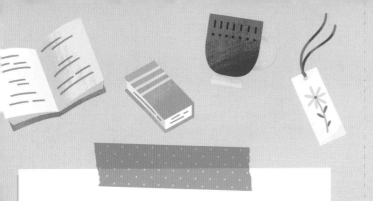

List of things I would prefer books over:

→ the movie version

→ people

→ reality

→ work

→ sleep

→ magazines

→ social engagements

→ the internet

→ money

so ... everything?

The **BOOK** *was* **BETTER.**

A Great Love of Books and Their Nooks

Are your bookshelves full? Has your collection expanded to take over every room, nook, and cranny in the house? You may wonder if you are experiencing *bibliomania*—the obsessive hoarding of books—or maybe just *bibliophilia*, a healthy and deep love of books.

In Japanese, there is a word for the act of buying reading materials and letting them pile up, without reading them: *tsundoku*.

Go on—let them stack up with abandon, just as long as you don't hide away your stash of books from the world—then you're a *bibliotaph*!

WISE OWLS READ

Oulysses

THE HOOT OF THE WILD

OF
MICE
AND
VOLES

OWL BE HERE FOR YOU

librocubicularist

(noun) *lih bro cyu BIH cyu luh rist*

someone who reads books in bed

Christopher Morley coined this term in his 1919 novel, The Haunted Bookshop.

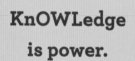

KnOWLedge
is power.

Can you match these novels with their authors?

Novels

The Remains of the Day

Oryx and Crake

White Teeth

Violeta

Giovanni's Room

Authors

Isabel Allende

Kazuo Ishiguro

James Baldwin

Zadie Smith

Margaret Atwood

(Turn the page for the answers!)

(Turn the page for the answers!)

LET'S GET LITERARY

Answers:

The Remains of the Day ➜ Kazuo Ishiguro

Oryx and Crake ➜ Margaret Atwood

White Teeth ➜ Zadie Smith

Violeta ➜ Isabel Allende

Giovanni's Room ➜ James Baldwin

My exercise is
reading in bed until
my arms hurt.

I WORK TO
SUPPORT MY
BOOK HABIT

Life is short—
read what you love.

The Oldest Bookstore in Operation

The Bertrand bookshop first opened in 1732 in Lisbon, Portugal. If you buy a book there, it can be stamped to prove that it was purchased at the world's oldest bookstore!

Library:

Author:

Title:

Date:	Name:	

ARC N BOOK
Seoul, South Korea

THE STRAND
New York City, USA

ATLANTIS BOOKS
Santorini, Greece

BOEKHANDEL DOMINICANEN
Maastrricht, Netherlands

Great Indie Bookstores

SHAKESPEARE AND COMPANY
Paris, France

EL ATENEO GRAND SPLENDID
Buenos Aires, Argentina

POWELL'S BOOKS
Portland, Oregon, USA

LIVRRARIA LELLO
Porto, Portugal

Between the pages of a book is a lovely place to be.

Bibliophile Problems

glasses

heavy tote bags

too many books,
too little time

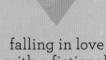

falling in love
with a fictional
character

paper
cuts

crying
in public

BOOK
·•· NERDS ·•·
UNITE!

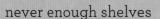

never enough shelves

The Many Names for Book Lovers

The word "bookworm" first appeared in the year 1580, according to the *Oxford English Dictionary*. It was likely not a friendly term at first—evoking bugs that inhabit and chow down on books.

When translated to other languages, "bookworm" becomes:

→ reading horse (Norwegian)

→ book maggot (Albanian, Turkish)

→ library mouse or rat (French, Italian, Portuguese, Romanian, Spanish)

→ book fool (Chinese)

→ book eater (Greek)

→ reading madness (Korean)

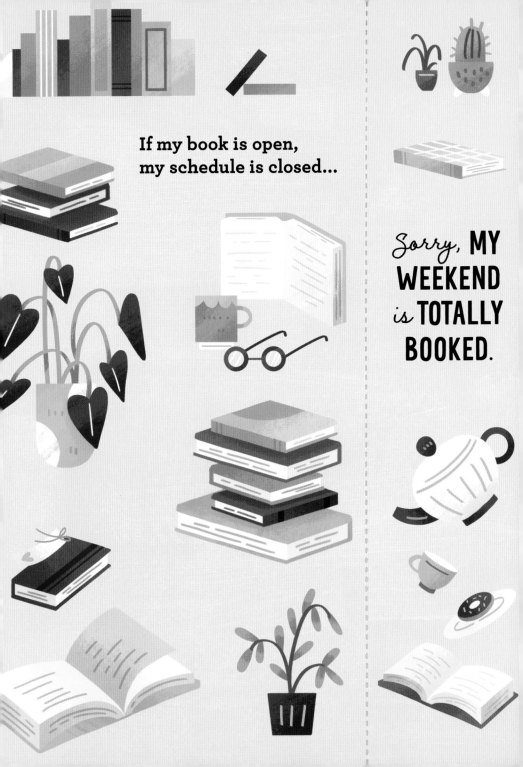

If my book is open,
my schedule is closed...

Sorry, MY WEEKEND is TOTALLY BOOKED.

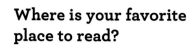

Where is your favorite place to read?

- ❏ in bed
- ❏ in a comfy living room chair
- ❏ on a park bench
- ❏ at a bar
- ❏ in a hammock
- ❏ on a train
- ❏ in an airplane
- ❏ next to a roaring fire
- ❏ on a sunny patch of grass
- ❏ in the tub
- ❏ on the toilet
- ❏ in the library
- ❏ next to your favorite person

The Care & Feeding of Books

Books enjoy...

→ being dusted

→ having their pages flipped through

→ moving around to different parts of the house

→ being loaned to loving friends

→ sitting upright or being fully supported

→ being the subject of a book club

BE TRUE
TO YOUR
SHELF.

I CAN
&
I WILL

Above
All else.
Be
Kind.

Self-Care Ideas that Pair Well with Books

Reading

- ❏ on the beach
- ❏ outside in nature
- ❏ while taking a bath

Listening to an audiobook

- ❏ while walking
- ❏ as you prepare a nourishing meal
- ❏ while cleaning the house
- ❏ as you fold the laundry

Sharing a book

- ❏ with a cup of coffee or tea
- ❏ while curled up with a pet
- ❏ with a friend

READING IS MY SUPER POWER.

The Pros and Cons of Reading

Pros

READING...

→   may increase lifespan

→   builds vocabulary

→   sharpens vision

→   helps with decision-making

→   decreases stress

→   lengthens attention span

→   sparks creativity

(continued on next page)

The Pros and Cons of Reading (cont'd)

Cons

READING...

→ may prevent you from attending social events

→ might deplete your budget

→ will make you feel emotions

book hangover

(noun phrase) *BOOK - HANG oh vuhr*

1. when you are unable to cope with the fact that your book is over

2. the sleep deprivation that comes with staying up too late to finish a book

READ

EAT

SLEEP

REPEAT

We lose ourselves in books and we find ourselves there, too.

"That's *the* thing *about* books.
They *let you* travel without
moving *your* feet."
—JHUMPA LAHIRI

Books *are the*
plane, *and the* train,
and the road. They *are*
the destination, *and the*
journey. They *are* home.

—ANNA QUINDLEN

Three Types of "Currently Reading" Piles

one book
at a time

fiction and
nonfiction

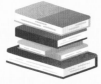

simultaneously
five books at once,
varying degrees of enthusiasm

Four Ways to Get Your Book Fix

library
loan

hardcover pre-order

second-hand
score

waiting until
paperback

Three People You Meet at Book Club

THE SECOND-CHANCE GIVER

leaves the book
for a month and
comes back later

THE PERSISTENT

reads every book
all the way through

THE ONE WITH CLEAR BOUNDARIES

believes that life
is too short to
read boring books

Reading Awakens the Senses

If you're someone with *bibliosima*, you love the scent of books—especially that musty, grassy odor that fills the air of an old bookshop.

As books get older (and more loved), they break down a bit. Chemical degradation of decaying glue, paper, and ink creates the release of volatile organic compounds— and a smell! Similar to a hint of vanilla, that precious scent occurs due to the breakdown of lignin, a supportive material in plant tissue and close relative of vanillin. And the smell has a name: *biblichor*.

Do you know the answers to these questions on writers and their process?

a) Which author wrote his last novel in crayon?

b) Where did Maya Angelou like to write?

c) Who famously wrote a book about the need for women to have their own physical and metaphorical space to write?

Answers:

a) James Joyce wrote *Ulysses* in red crayon on large sheets of paper due to severe impairment of his vision.

b) Maya Angelou wrote in a hotel room with a bottle of sherry, a dictionary, a deck of cards, and the Bible next to her.

c) Virginia Woolf in *A Room of One's Own*.

Keep track of your reading—fill in this page and the bookmark with the titles of each book you've read!

AUTHOR	TITLE	DATE COMPLETED

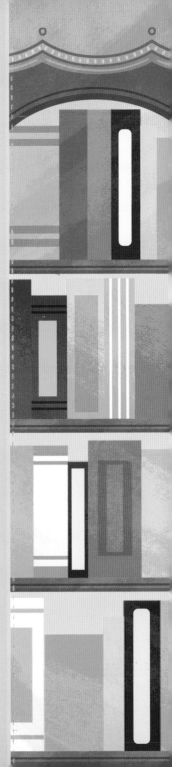

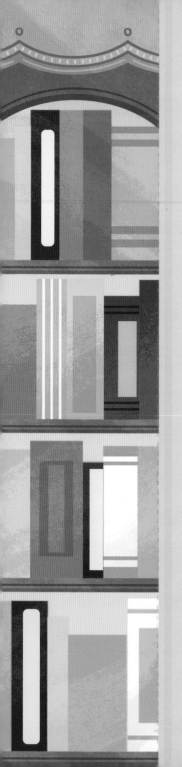

AUTHOR	TITLE	DATE COMPLETED